Space Technology
Shuttles
by Julie Murray
Dash!
LEVELED READERS
An Imprint of Abdo Zoom • abdobooks.com
3

Level 1 – Beginning
Short and simple sentences with familiar words or patterns for children who are beginning to understand how letters and sounds go together.

Level 2 – Emerging
Longer words and sentences with more complex language patterns for readers who are practicing common words and letter sounds.

Level 3 – Transitional
More developed language and vocabulary for readers who are becoming more independent.

abdobooks.com

Published by Abdo Zoom, a division of ABDO, PO Box 398166, Minneapolis, Minnesota 55439.
Copyright © 2020 by Abdo Consulting Group, Inc. International copyrights reserved in all countries.
No part of this book may be reproduced in any form without written permission from the publisher.
Dash!™ is a trademark and logo of Abdo Zoom.

Printed in the United States of America, North Mankato, Minnesota.
102019
012020

Photo Credits: iStock, Depositphotos Enterprise, NASA, NASA/Bill Ingalls, NASA/Frank Michaux
Production Contributors: Kenny Abdo, Jennie Forsberg, Grace Hansen, John Hansen
Design Contributors: Dorothy Toth, Neil Klinepier, Victoria Bates

Library of Congress Control Number: 2019941336

Publisher's Cataloging in Publication Data

Names: Murray, Julie, author.
Title: Shuttles / by Julie Murray
Description: Minneapolis, Minnesota : Abdo Zoom, 2020 | Series: Space technology | Includes online resources and index.
Identifiers: ISBN 9781532129292 (lib. bdg.) | ISBN 9781098220273 (ebook) | ISBN 9781098220761 (Read-to-Me ebook)
Subjects: LCSH: Space shuttles--Juvenile literature. | Rocket ships--Juvenile literature. | Space sciences--Juvenile literature. | Technology--Juvenile literature. | Space travel--Juvenile literature.
Classification: DDC 629.441--dc23

Table of Contents

Shuttles

Shuttles carry crew members, **satellites**, and equipment into space. They are reusable spacecraft.

A shuttle takes off like a rocket. It **orbits** around Earth like a **satellite**. It lands like an airplane.

Parts of a
Shuttle

There are three main parts of
a shuttle. The orbiter is where
the crew lives and works. It
holds the main engines. It
also has wings.

The external tank carries liquid hydrogen and oxygen. It fuels the engines during take-off. It breaks off and **descends** back to Earth. Some parts burn up. Others fall into the ocean.

The rocket boosters push the orbiter and external tank into space. After take-off, they detach and fall back to Earth. Parachutes glide the boosters into the ocean. They are recovered and reused.

Space Shuttle
Program
14

The National Aeronautics and Space Administration (NASA) ran the Space Shuttle Program from 1981 to 2011. It had five space-worthy shuttles during this time. *Columbia* was the first. It ran for 22 years and completed 27 missions. Sadly, it burned up upon reentry in 2003. All seven crew members died.

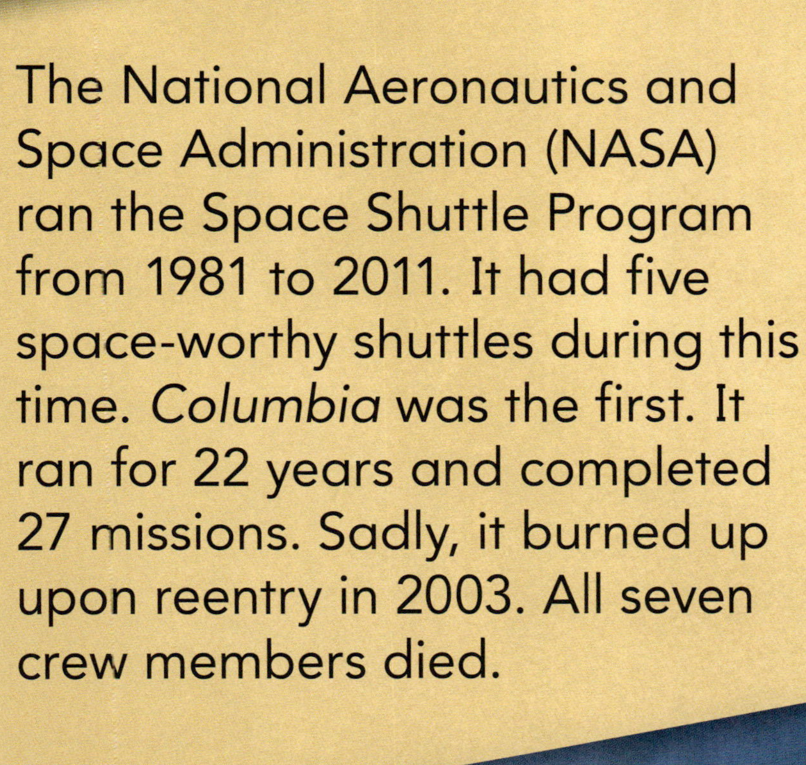

Challenger was NASA's second shuttle. It flew from 1983 to 1986, when it broke apart during take-off. All seven crew members were tragically lost. The third was *Discovery*. It flew 39 missions from 1984 to 2011.

USA
NASA
Challenger

United States
We Made
Atlan

Atlantis was the fourth shuttle. It flew 33 missions from 1985 to 2011. It flew the last mission for the Space Shuttle Program. *Endeavour*, the fifth shuttle, flew 25 missions from 1992 to 2011.

Space shuttles played an important role in building the **International Space Station (ISS)**. They delivered important parts to the ISS during construction. They also transported many crew members to and from the ISS.

- *Enterprise* was also a shuttle. It was only made for test flights in the atmosphere.

- Between 1981 and 2011, 135 successful shuttle missions were flown.

- A total of 355 different astronauts have flown on a space shuttle. F. Story Musgrave is the only one to fly aboard all five shuttles.

Glossary

descend – to move downward.

International Space Station (ISS) – a large spacecraft in orbit around Earth. It serves as a home and science laboratory where crews of astronauts live and work. Several nations worked together to build it.

orbit – (n) the curved path in which a natural or artificial body moves in a circle around a star, planet, or moon. (v) to move in a circle around.

satellite – an artificial body placed in orbit around Earth, a moon, or another planet in order to collect information or for communication.

Index

Online Resources

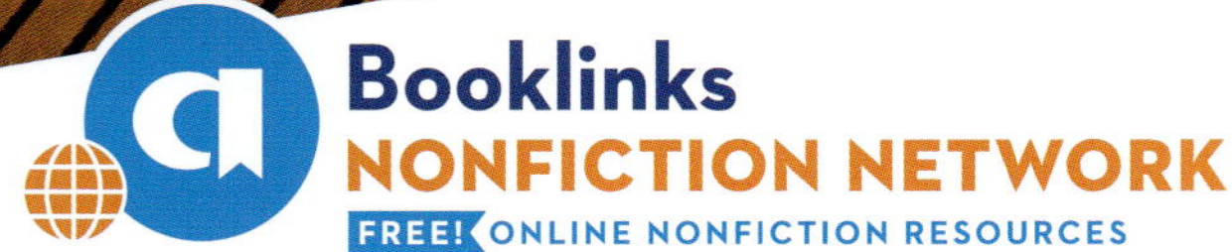

GET INVOLVED IN AN E-SPORTS CLUB!

BY CHRISTINA MAJASKI

CAPSTONE PRESS
a capstone imprint

Published by Capstone Press, an imprint of Capstone.
1710 Roe Crest Drive, North Mankato, Minnesota 56003
capstonepub.com

Library of Congress Cataloging-in-Publication Data is available on the Library of Congress website.

ISBN: 9781663958846 (hardcover)
ISBN: 9781666320459 (ebook PDF)

Summary: Excited about e-sports? If so, an e-sports club might be the right fit for you! Find out what it takes to join an e-sports club or start your own, including information on membership, meetings, and activities. Together, you and your fellow members can participate, create, and, most importantly, have fun. Take the plunge, join the club, and get involved!

Editorial Credits
Editor: Ericka Smith; Designer: Sarah Bennett; Media Researcher: Svetlana Zhurkin; Production Specialist: Katy LaVigne

Image Credits
Getty Images: Ariel Skelley, 14, Chris Ryan, 9, JGI/Jamie Grill, cover (middle), 15, 29, kali9, 20, 22, Mike Stobe, 27, Neustockimages, 7, SDI Productions, 21; Shutterstock: Alex Tihonovs, 28, AllNikArt (doodles), cover background and throughout, Andrey_Popov, 12, Artgraphixel (blackboard), cover background and throughout, carballo, 4, HaseHoch2, 16, Jimena Roquero, 13, Maryna Terletska, 25, mijatmijatovic, 24, Monkey Business Images, 19, Mr.Whiskey, 18, OHishiapply, cover (top), 6, 11, Om.Nom.Nom, cover (bottom), releon8211, cover (top right), SewCream, 23, SSokolov, 8, tmcphotos, 5, Zivica Kerkez, 17

Printed and bound in the USA. PO#

TABLE OF CONTENTS

Words in **bold** are in the glossary.

GET IN THE GAME

If you like video games, you've probably heard of **e-sports**. Or maybe you've just heard about competitions involving video games. E-sports—or electronic sports—is the term used to describe video game competitions. If that sounds like something you're interested in, consider joining an e-sports club!

An e-sports club is a great way to hang out with your friends. You can also make new friends around the world. If you don't know anyone nearby who likes the same games as you, you'll probably find players online who do.

There are hundreds of e-sports games and clubs. If you can't find a club that matches your interests, start your own!

CHAPTER 1

ABOUT E-SPORTS CLUBS

An e-sports club is a group of video game players who practice and compete together. Think of it like a basketball team, but for video games! You and your fellow club members need to practice your gaming skills and learn how to work together to succeed.

And just like in athletic sports, competing in
e-sports is challenging and exciting. You test your
skills and creativity under pressure. One spectacular
move could make all the difference for your team.

Types of E-sports Clubs

There's a club for nearly every **genre**—or type—of game. Common types include **real-time strategy games** and **multiplayer online battle arena games**. *League of Legends* is an example of a popular multiplayer online battle arena game.

Benefits of an E-sports Club

There are many benefits of being in an e-sports club. First, you can focus on your favorite games. You can also learn about new games and **strategies** from others. And e-sports clubs give you a chance to build friendships with people who have similar interests.

So look around and find an e-sports club where you can play your favorite games with other kids. Or start your own!

Joining an E-sports Club

If you'd like to join an e-sports club, see what's available in your area. Many schools are forming e-sports clubs. You should also check for statewide and national clubs.

To join a large club, you'll have to meet some requirements. You might need to have specific gaming skills. And just like a job, you will probably need to apply. Big teams are generally looking for members with the skills to help them win **tournaments.**

You may also have to pay a fee to join an e-sports club. The cost might be limited to extra events, like participating in competitions. Some established statewide and nationwide e-sports clubs cost around $35 a month. This fee covers unlimited access to **leagues** and games.

Tip: If you're joining a school-sponsored club, there might not be a fee. Start there and see what you find!

STARTING YOUR OWN E-SPORTS CLUB

If you can't find a club to join, you may want to start one. To start your own e-sports club, you'll need to decide a few basic things. First, identify which type of e-sports club you want to start. Here are some popular types:

- fighting games

- multiplayer online battle arena games

- racing games

- sports games

- card games

- real-time strategy games

Once you've chosen a type of club to start, think about the purpose of your club. Do you want to develop your skills in a particular game? Will you prepare for a competition?

After you've decided your club's purpose, start thinking more about the details. What **guidelines** will you have for membership? What rules will members have to follow? Deciding these details will help you find members and plan your meetings.

Membership Guidelines

The most important guideline for membership should be an interest in e-sports. But it might be helpful to set some other guidelines. For example, do you want to set an age range for members? If you're starting a club at school, can students who don't attend your school join? Do you want to have members with different experience levels so that you can learn from one another?

Rules and Responsibilities

What other rules will you have? Should meetings be required? What happens if a member breaks a rule? For example, if someone misses three meetings, can they still compete?

Also think about your members' responsibilities. Are there **dues**? Will members need to bring any equipment to meetings?

Finding Members

Not sure where to find members? E-sports games are very popular. It might surprise you how many people nearby are playing the same games you are.

Start looking for members in your community. Talk to kids you know at school. Hang posters in your neighborhood. You might have a full club in no time!

Try It! Make a Poster

Create a poster about the type of club you want to start. Include the date, time, and location for your first meeting, as well as your contact information.

Ask if you can hang the posters around your school or neighborhood. You can also post in online gaming groups if you want to open up membership to people outside of your area. Ask a trusted adult to help you post the information in your community and online.

You can use this sample poster as a guide.

Assigning Roles

Clubs sometimes have leadership **roles**. People share the work of making sure a club runs smoothly. Having set roles might also help if you want to plan a lot of activities. Some common roles are:

- president—leads meetings and plans activities

- vice president—helps the president

- secretary—takes notes at meetings

- treasurer—keeps track of money raised

You can discuss these roles at your first club meeting. Or you can have members volunteer to take care of certain duties.

Adult Sponsor and Safety

You'll need an adult to be a **sponsor** for your club. This should be a trusted adult, like a parent or teacher. This person helps you make decisions and plan activities. They can also help you with tasks, like posting flyers for your club and handling membership dues.

Because e-sports clubs take place online, your sponsor or another adult should be around when you're playing or competing. Even if your club only has members from your school, when you play against other teams, you probably won't know everyone. (And you won't always know who you are playing with online.) Your sponsor can step in to help if you feel concerned.

Club Costs

An e-sports club may have some costs. You might need to pay for equipment like headphones. Or maybe you'll have to pay entry fees for competitions.

You can do things to raise money. You might have members pay dues. Or you might choose to **fundraise**. Cleaning up yards in your neighborhood or selling baked goods are both good fundraising ideas.

Some major e-sports clubs have businesses that help them cover their costs. Those businesses are called sponsors too. You don't have to be a professional to get sponsors. See if any businesses in your area will sponsor your club.

CLUB MEETINGS

You may not need to meet regularly in an e-sports club. You'll likely spend a lot of your time online practicing and learning new strategies. However, you will need to have some meetings to discuss what's happening with your club.

At your first meeting, you'll need to take care of a few things:

- Choose a club name.

- Assign club duties.

- Pick a day and time to meet.

- Decide where to meet.

- Set goals.

Choose a Name

First, work together to decide on a name for your club. You can use things club members have in common to come up with a name. Or focus on what types of games your club likes to play.

Assign Club Duties

Talk with members about whether your club will have leadership roles. If you decide to have leadership roles, members can volunteer for a particular role. Or you might decide to have members vote on who should fill a role at a later meeting.

Schedule Regular Meetings

Decide on a day and time for your club to meet. Do you want to meet once a month? Or would you rather meet once a week?

Settle on a time that works best for everyone. You can always change the days and times later based on things like summer vacation or the new school year.

Select a Location

Decide where your club will meet. Consider meeting at members' homes or the library. You might be able to meet at your school. Just be sure to get permission from your principal. If you're not sure where you can meet, ask your sponsor for suggestions.

One of the benefits of an e-sports club is you don't necessarily have to meet in person. Many clubs meet online, using programs like Zoom. As long as your computer has a camera, members can still see each other.

 Set Up a Zoom Meeting

You can set up a Zoom meeting with a computer or a phone. Have an adult, like your sponsor, help you create an account and schedule a meeting for your club. You can schedule just one meeting, or you can schedule several meetings at once if you want to meet regularly. Once you've added the information for the meeting in Zoom, send the link or phone number to your members.

Meeting Agendas

An **agenda** is a list of the things you will do during a meeting. It will help your club meetings run smoothly. An agenda can be a useful tool to make sure you cover everything at each meeting. It will also be a record of what you did in case you need a reminder later.

On a sheet of paper, make a list of things you want to accomplish at your meeting and how long each one will take. Make sure the agenda includes the meeting date and time, plus a space to list the members who are at the meeting. Also include a section for filling in any club challenges or questions you need to address, such as ideas for getting members. Use the sample agenda below as a guide.

Mark Elementary E-sports Club

Thursday, Sept. 30, 4:00 p.m.

4:00 p.m.   Announcements

4:10 p.m.   Challenges and Questions

     1.

     2.

     3.

4:30 p.m.   Strategy Discussion: Using the walls in *Rocket League*

Members present: Susan, Thomas, Nyla, Felix, Jackie, Marcus, Maria

Setting Goals

Discuss some possible goals with club members at your first meeting. This will help you plan meetings and activities for your club. For example, do you want to set a goal for your club members' level in a particular game? If so, you might practice certain strategies during club meetings.

COMPETITIONS, TOURNAMENTS, AND LEAGUES

Competitions are a big part of e-sports. Your club may decide to enter a competition right away. Or it might be something you're interested in doing later.

If you decide to enter a competition, check for local tournaments. You can search for these online. Make sure to ask an adult—like your sponsor—to help you enter.

Popular E-sports Leagues

There are many e-sports leagues around the world. Here are a few popular ones that you can follow:

- **Overwatch League:** This league is for *Overwatch* fans and fans of other Blizzard Entertainment games. It includes teams from all over the world. You might be able to find one from your area.

Big Prizes Tournaments are a big deal in e-sports. Some of the most famous ones include the International, the Overwatch World Cup, and the Fortnite World Cup. The 2019 Fortnite World Cup Finals awarded prizes totaling $33.6 million. The 2019 Dota 2 International 9 tournament awarded prizes totaling $34.3 million.

- **Call of Duty League:** This league was started in 2020. It includes twelve teams from four countries.

- **Rocket League Championship Series:** This tournament series is organized by Psyonix, the game's creator. People in North America, South America, Europe, and Oceania can participate.

Celebrate Your Hard Work

You've learned new strategies and practiced playing your favorite games. Maybe you've even entered competitions with your club. Take some time to celebrate your hard work! You might throw a pizza party or have a game night at a club member's home. You can do this at the end of the year or school year— or after a competition.

With hundreds of e-sports clubs forming, and tournaments taking place all over the world, it's easy to get involved with e-sports. Join a club or start your own. You just need to have an interest in video games and a way to connect with other gamers in your area or around the world. Before you know it, you'll be gaming with old and new friends!

GLOSSARY

agenda (uh-JEN-duh)—a list of things to be done or talked about

dues (DOOZ)—regular charges or fees for club members

e-sports (EE-sports)—electronic sports or multiplayer video games

fundraise (FUHND-rayz)—to raise money for a project by doing things like asking for donations or selling things

genre (ZHAHN-ruh)—a class or category

guideline (GYD-line)—a rule for how to do something

league (LEEG)—a group of teams that play against each other

multiplayer online battle arena game (MUHL-tee-play-ur ON-line BA-tuhl uh-REE-nuh GAYM)—a video game in which players control characters and battle as a team to control a specific space, or arena, within the game

real-time strategy game (REEL-time STRA-tuh-jee GAYM)—a video game in which players control a variety of military units and resources to defeat opponents

role (ROHL)—a person's job and duties

sponsor (SPON-sur)—a person responsible for something; also a company or organization that gives an individual or team equipment or money to participate in a competition

strategy (STRA-tuh-jee)—a plan for winning a game or contest

tournament (TUR-nuh-muhnt)—a series of matches between several players or teams, ending in one winner

READ MORE

Gregory, Josh. *History of Esports*. Ann Arbor, MI: Cherry Lake Publishing, 2020.

Mauleón, Daniel. *Esports Revolution*. North Mankato, MN: Capstone Press, 2020.

Owings, Lisa. *The World of Esports*. Minneapolis: Lerner, 2021.

INTERNET SITES

Connected Camps: "Free Minecraft Club Server"
connectedcamps.com/minecraft-kid-club

International Esports Federation
iesf.org

North America Scholastic Esports Federation
nasef.org

INDEX

ABOUT THE AUTHOR

Christina Majaski is a digital media and personal finance writer based in central Minnesota, where she lives with her dog, Monty, and her daughter, Chloe. She has covered games such as *Minecraft* and *Roblox* in both online and print publications for more than a decade.